DEALING WITH

FAMILY CHANGES

STEPH GIEDD

childsworld.com

The Child's World
childsworld.com

Published by The Child's World®
800-599-READ • www.childsworld.com

Photography Credits
Photographs ©: Wavebreak Media/iStockphoto, cover, 1, 9, 18–19; Orbon Alija/iStockphoto, 5; iStockphoto, 6, 11, 13, 14, 17, 22; Shutterstock Images, 20

ISBN Information
9781503885417 (Reinforced Library Binding)
9781503885592 (Portable Document Format)
9781503886230 (Online Multi-user eBook)
9781503886872 (Electronic Publication)

LCCN 2023937432

Printed in the United States of America

BRINGING THE WORLD TO YOUNG READERS 1968

Steph Giedd is a former high school English teacher who now works as an editor. Originally from southern Iowa, Giedd lives in Minneapolis, Minnesota, with her husband, daughter, and pets.

TABLE OF CONTENTS

CHAPTER 1

When Family Changes Happen

Sometimes big changes happen within families. This can include a new person coming into a family. For example, parents might bring home a new sibling. Other times, families change when parents get divorced. Families also change when a parent gets remarried. This brings in a new stepparent and maybe even stepsiblings.

Getting a new sibling can be exciting, but it may also make kids feel like they are being replaced.

People experiencing the same change may have very different feelings.

Life may also change if a family member goes through a hard time. Some challenges affect the entire family. An example of this could be if a family member is hurt in a bad accident. They may need extra help after getting injured. The whole family might get new **responsibilities**.

There are many ways a family can change. The change could be good or bad. It can bring about **uncertainty**. It can cause **stress**, which can affect people both at home and at school. Changes can cause other strong feelings, too. For example, family members may feel happy, excited, or worried about getting a new sibling. They may feel angry, sad, or uncertain about a family member going through a hard time. They might even feel helpless. No matter how someone feels during a challenging or uncertain time, it is important to remember that all feelings are OK.

CHAPTER 2

Coping with Family Changes

Research shows that kids do best in a stable **household**. A stable household is one without constant changes. But when changes do happen, it is important to know how to handle them. There are different ways to get through big family changes.

Moving can lead to big changes, such as switching schools and leaving friends behind.

First, when a family change happens, people should ask questions. That way, there may be fewer surprises. Surprises can lead to uncertainty and stress.

Next, people should try to accept the change. If the change is positive, they can think about the good things that will happen because of it. For example, if a new sibling joins the family, there will be someone new to play with.

Other changes may seem to have nothing good about them at all. Divorces and injuries can be scary and stressful. In these situations, it is important to find ways to deal with stress. Some people exercise to help their bodies feel better.

Spending time with animals can lower stress.

Others may spend time with friends. This can help people feel supported. Others spend time in nature. This can help calm people's minds. Learning to handle stress makes changes easier.

When people are going through family changes, it is important for them to talk about their feelings. When people keep their feelings inside, they often feel worse. Strong emotions can make it hard to do everyday things, such as paying attention in school or sleeping. Talking about these feelings can make people feel better. People should share their feelings with a trusted adult or friend. People can also share their feelings with others who have gone through a similar life change. These people may have advice about how to cope.

Symptoms of Stress

Stress can affect how a person's body feels. Talking about one's feelings can make a person feel better.

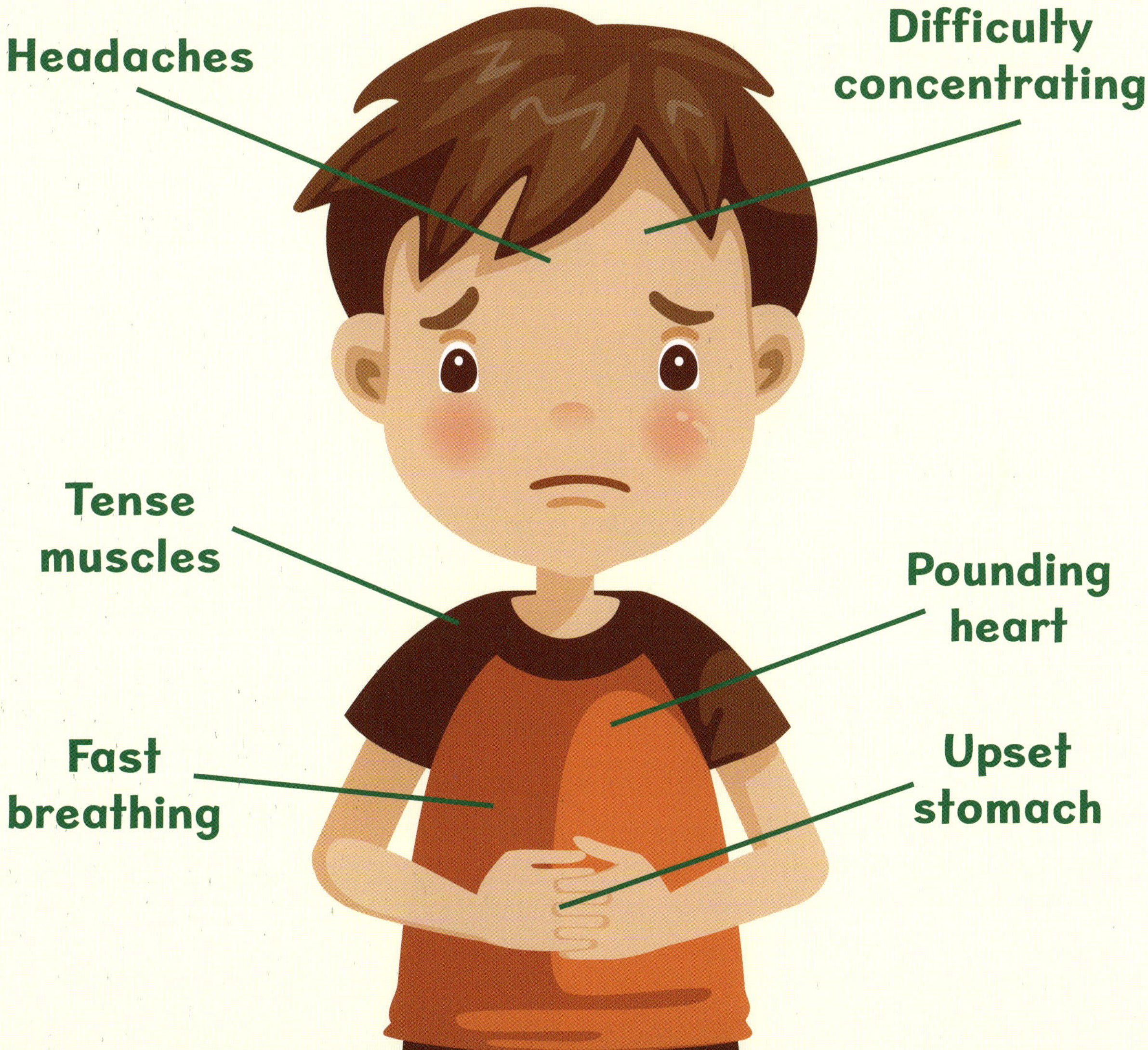

Talking to a trusted adult can help people work through strong emotions.

When the Country Calls

Sometimes families change when a family member joins the military. A parent or sibling going away to serve the country is a big change. It may even cause the family to move to another home. People going through this change can talk to a trusted adult or friend about their feelings.

Family changes can be hard for the whole family. It may make people sad to see their loved ones struggling. But there are ways to help them. For example, if there is a new sibling, parents might be very busy. Kids can help their parents by offering to do chores. They can take out the garbage. They can help with the new sibling by changing a diaper or folding the baby's laundry. Having a sense of purpose can help kids with uncertainty. Having a steady **routine** can also make changes feel more **manageable**.

CHAPTER 3

Helping a Friend Deal with Family Changes

Sometimes a friend may go through a big family change. It can be hard to know what to do or say to make the friend feel better. Whatever the friend is feeling, it's important to be supportive.

There are many ways to show support for a friend going through a family change. First, a person should be available to listen to the friend's feelings. It's important to not judge or **criticize** what the friend is saying or feeling.

It is important to support struggling friends.

Ask friends how to best support them, and be prepared to listen.

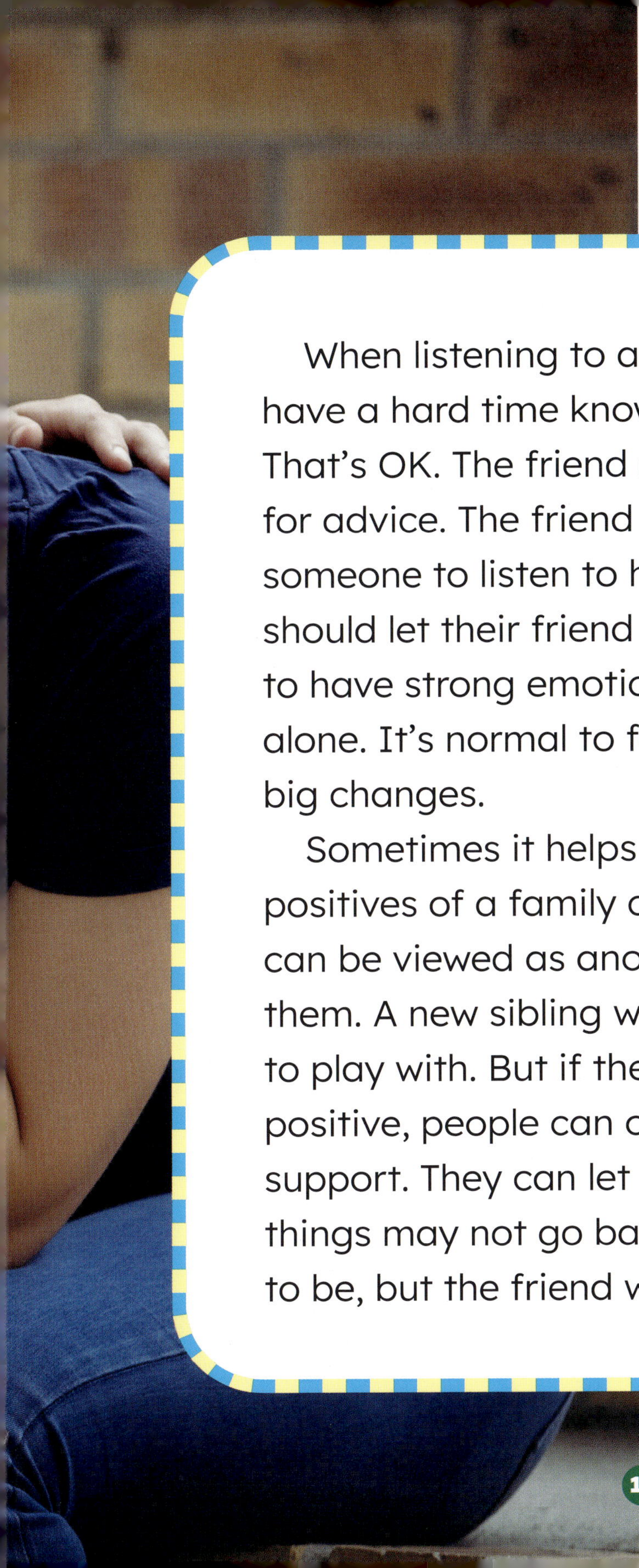

When listening to a friend, people might have a hard time knowing what to say. That's OK. The friend may not be looking for advice. The friend might simply want someone to listen to him or her. People should let their friend know that it's OK to have strong emotions. The friend isn't alone. It's normal to feel emotional during big changes.

Sometimes it helps to point out the positives of a family change. A new parent can be viewed as another person to love them. A new sibling will be another person to play with. But if the change isn't so positive, people can offer their friends support. They can let the friend know things may not go back to how they used to be, but the friend will get through it.

When people feel like they can talk about their feelings, it helps them feel less stressed. But sometimes they might not want to talk about the change. They might want to think about something else. People should pay attention to what their friends need. Sometimes being with people is enough to make friends feel better. They may feel supported just by knowing that someone cares.

Wonder More

Wondering about New Information

How much did you know about dealing with family changes before reading this book? What new information did you learn? Write down three new facts that this book taught you. Was the new information surprising? Why or why not?

Wondering How It Matters

What is one family change that has happened in your life? How did that affect you? If you haven't experienced a family change, think about your friends. Have they gone through a change in their families? What impact did it have on their lives?

Wondering Why

Why do you think it's important to learn about how to deal with family changes? How might learning about this topic help you?

Ways to Keep Wondering

There are many different types of family changes. After reading this book, what questions do you have about this topic? What can you do to learn more about how to deal with family changes?

Fast Facts

- A change in a family can include adding a stepparent or a new sibling. It can also include an injury or a divorce.
- Family changes may cause strong emotions. These emotions could be joy, anger, uncertainty, or sadness.
- Exercising, playing with friends, and being in nature are all good ways to cope with negative feelings.
- Asking for help and sharing feelings are ways to get rid of stress.
- Kids can help their families during big changes by taking on responsibilities.
- To be a good friend, it's important to listen without judging.
- After a big change, life may not go back to the way it used to be, but people can learn how to manage the new situation.

Glossary

criticize (KRIT-ih-size) To criticize means to tell people that they are wrong. When listening to struggling friends, try not to criticize them.

household (HOWSS-hohld) A household is a group of people who live together. Adding a baby to a household can create a lot of changes.

manageable (MAN-ij-uh-bul) Something that can be dealt with is manageable. Talking about one's feelings can make stressful situations seem more manageable.

responsibilities (reh-spon-sih-BIL-uh-teez) Responsibilities are things one has to do. When families change, responsibilities change, too.

routine (roo-TEEN) A routine is a set of things that someone does regularly. When big changes happen, following a routine can make life seem more normal.

stress (STRESS) If someone is very worried, he or she is experiencing stress. Spending time with friends is one way to get rid of stress.

uncertainty (uhn-SUR-tuhn-tee) People deal with uncertainty when they are unsure about something. Big changes can create uncertainty because people may not know what will happen next.

Find Out More

In the Library

An, Priscilla. *Mindfulness with Family.* Parker, CO: The Child's World, 2024.

Giedd, Steph. *Dealing with Divorce.* Parker, CO: The Child's World, 2024.

Miller, Marie-Therese. *Families Like Mine.* Minneapolis, MN: Lerner, 2021.

On the Web

Visit our website for links about dealing with family changes:
childsworld.com/links

Note to Parents, Caregivers, Teachers, and Librarians: We routinely verify our Web links to make sure they are safe and active sites. So encourage your readers to check them out!

Index